This book belongs to:

. . . .

Rainbows & Storms
Copyright © Jennifer Jackson and Nisha Jaime

For information contact:

Jennifer Jackson: jenrainbowsandstorms@gmail.com
Nisha Jaime: nisharainbowsandstorms@gmail.com

Self-published and written by Dr. Jennifer Jackson and Nisha Jaime
Illustrations copyright © Anna Scheckel

ISBN 978-1-7368164-0-0
Made in the USA, 2021

Rainbows & Storms

Written for our heart warriors, Layla & Nylah, whose paths crossed because of congenital heart disease.

Written by:

Dr.Jennifer Jackson and Nisha Jaime

Illustrated by:

Anna Scheckel

Two little girls both smiley and sweet,
crossed paths one day with the same heartbeat.

You would never guess CHD was their norm,
that caused them to face both rainbows and storms.

Different hearts you might say, yet the path is the same ...
these two little friends with a big fight and aim.

Faith, hope and love carries them through,
with family and friends whose love remains true.

They are strong and courageous as they battle the fight, remembering who they are and keeping their bond tight.

Their mommies tell them their hearts are the route,
to following their dreams and to helping others out.

Their defect does not define them, their choices remain. They embrace their uniqueness and see themselves as the same.

When they encounter mean words or mistreatment from others, they return to each other for kindness and wonders.

Love is the way when you are faced with something hard ... trust in each other because your beauty is your scar!

Dr. Jennifer Jackson

Dr. Jennifer Jackson is a devoted mother to a daughter who was born with congenital heart disease. This journey, alongside her career in education, makes her passionate about positively impacting the lives of young people. Jennifer is a Los Angeles-based educator having served previously as a secondary teacher turned administrator.

Nisha Jaime

Nisha Jaime is a doting mama to twin boys and a daughter who was born with the congenital heart disease, Tetralogy of Fallot. Nisha is a Los Angeles-based journalist who has had a love for writing since she was a little girl.

Anna Scheckel

Anna Scheckel is a Pasadena-based artist who believes that art should always be used as a medium for understanding and change. With a degree in Studio Art from Drew University, she hopes to achieve just that.

What is a CHD?

Congenital Heart Disease, also referred to as CHD, is a term used to describe a wide range of abnormalities that affect the heart. A CHD occurs as a baby's heart is developing during pregnancy. In the United States, approximately 40,000 babies are born every year with a CHD and 25% of them will need heart surgery or other interventions to survive, according to the Centers for Disease Control and Prevention. There is currently no cure for CHD. Many cases are complex and require ongoing specialized cardiac care.

For those who are a parent or caregiver to a heart warrior with a CHD, we would like to personally recommend the following organizations for you to contact for support and resources:

Save the Heartbeat
2247 Lindsay Way, Glendora, CA 91740
Danielle Maloof, Founder
www.savetheheartbeat.org
Facebook/Instagram/Twitter: @SavetheHeartbeat

Bright Heart Foundation
P.O. Box 3463, Brentwood, TN 37024
Clint & Linda Pilkinton, Founders
(615) 873-0152
Email: info@BrightHeartFoundation.org
www.BrightHeartFoundation.org
Facebook/Instagram: @BrightHeartFoundation

Conquering CHD
Email: info@conqueringchd.org
www.conqueringchd.org
Facebook/Instagram/Twitter: @conqueringchd

Thank You